Animal Lullabies

Animal Lullabies

PAM CONRAD

RICHARD COWDREY

A LAURA GERINGER BOOK
An Imprint of HarperCollins Publishers

Animal Lullabies

Text copyright © 1997 by the Estate of Pamela Conrad

Illustrations copyright © 1997 by Richard Cowdrey

Printed in the U.S.A. All rights reserved.

Library of Congress Cataloging-in-Publication Data

Conrad, Pam.

Animal lullabies / by Pam Conrad; illustrated by Richard Cowdrey.   p.   cm.

Summary: As the day draws to a close, animal parents, from giraffes to oysters, guard and hush

their offspring in this collection of bedtime poems.

ISBN 0-06-024718-5. — ISBN 0-06-024719-3 (lib. bdg.)

1. Parent and child—Juvenile poetry.   2. Animals—Juvenile poetry.   3. Children's poetry,

American.   4. Lullabies, American.   [1. Parent and child—Poetry.   2. Animals—Poetry.

3. American poetry.   4. Lullabies.]   I. Cowdrey, Richard, ill.   II. Title.

PS3553.05185A8   1997   96-23210   811'.54—dc20   CIP   AC

1   2   3   4   5   6   7   8   9   10   ❖   First Edition

To my wife, Cindy,

for all her love, support, and encouragement

—R

Giraffe Lullaby

On the peaceful savanna
a giraffe whispers to her nephew—
"Keep still, my sweetheart,
your momma will be back."

The skinny child stretches high
out of the acacia leaves.
But is the lion coming?
Where are the zebras tonight?

She swats her long tasseled tail
and casts her lidded eyes about.
Wind rustles the secret grass.
"Be still, my sweetheart,
your momma's on her way."

Alligator Lullaby

"Stay away from my darling or I'll eat you alive!"
roars the mother crocodile,
afloat like a log in oil.
She slaps her tail on the black river.
"Stay away now or I'll eat you alive!"

Her sharp white teeth grin bright in the dark.
Her eyes seem almost closed.
See her sweet darling balanced on her nose,
dreaming sleepy lagoon dreams?
"Stay away now or I'll eat you alive!"

Squirrel Lullaby

"Come. Come up now
and see what I've made for you.
A bed of leaves
where you can sleep."

"What? What is it?
Something for me?"

"Momma loves your squirrel fur,
moonlight shining through your tail.
But come here now. Settle down.
And see what I've made for you."

"What? What is it?
What have you got?
Something for me?"

"Yes, come see. Settle down.
See what I have?
See what I've made for you?"

Oyster Lullaby

The sea is deep and dark at night.
"Clat. Clat. Clatty dunk.
Time to close up tight."

The starfish shimmers, glimmers
along the shadow-blue floor.
"Time, my dears, to close up tight,
close your doors and lock the bolts.
Spin your pearls before it's light!"

The sea is deep and dark at night.
"Clat. Clat. Clatty dunk.
Spin your pearls, so white."

Beaver Lullaby

SLAP! SLAP! WHACKUM!
SLAP! SLAP! WHACKUM!

Murky blue pond,
in the middle of a bog.
A beaver calls.

Away from the lodge
her children roll in the mud.
They don't answer.

"Let's wash those faces.
Wipe those feet.
Come on home to me!"

SLAP! SLAP! WHACKUM!
goes her tail and *whisk* —
her kits come running —

SLAP! SLAP! WHACKUM!
SLAP! SLAP! WHACKUM!
"Come on home to me."

Swan Lullaby

"Once more around the lake.
Around, around.
Once more before we go."

Circling a wide moon,
the swanlings grow tired.
Their mother watches
from sleepy eyes.

"Oh, moon, oh, stars.
Once more around the lake.
Around, around.
Once more so that you sleep."

Prairie Dog Lullaby

Prairie dog —
half in, half out of her hole —
hums a tune as a blade of grass
casts its long shadow.

She hums, "Hush, it's only darkness.
Hush, it's just the wind."

Prairie pups nestle
and her humming swirls about them
like dust devils, like moon light,
like tumbleweed passing through cottonwood.

"Hush, it's only darkness.
Hush, it's just the wind."

Sea Horse Lullaby

"Gather! Come gather!
Such dangers abound!
Gather! Come gather
in seaweed with me!"

In seaweed grasses
a gallant sea horse
hangs on with his tail.

His children
never close their eyes.
Never sleep at all.

And *never* listen,
but flick their small fins
and scatter seaweed
everywhere.

"Gather! Come gather!
Such dangers abound!
Gather! Come gather
in seaweed with me!"

Monkey Lullaby

Daddy says: "And tonight
Baby's sleeping with me
for rocking and hugging,
here in the banyan tree
so high."

Momma steals the baby.
"No, Baby sleeps with me,
in my long furry arms
where the milk is so fresh
and warm."

And Cousin swoops Baby
off and says: "Oh, Baby's
gotta sleep with me and
we'll watch the sun set down
so fast."

And Grandma too, she says:
"I need a babe tonight
for cooings and kissings,
beneath the gibbous moon
so bright."

But Daddy says again:
"Ohhh, no, Baby's with me!
You all know it's my turn."
And Baby smiles and smiles
and smiles.

Owl's Lullaby to Her Daughter

Wake up, wake up, my soft owl child.

The moon is growing fat.

Follow me, follow me, low here and swift.

Wake up, wake up my soft owl child.

The moon, it lights our way!